Amazing World
of Science and Math

MATH
ADDS UP

LISA REGAN

Gareth Stevens
PUBLISHING

Please visit our website, www.garethstevens.com.
For a free color catalog of all our high-quality books,
call toll free 1-800-542-2595 or fax 1-877-542-2596.

Cataloging-in-Publication Data
Names: Regan, Lisa.
Title: Math adds up / Lisa Regan.
Description: New York : Gareth Stevens Publishing, 2017. | Series: Amazing world of science
  and math | Includes index.
Identifiers: ISBN 9781482449860 (pbk.) | ISBN 9781482449884 (library bound) |
  ISBN 9781482449877 (6 pack)
Subjects: LCSH: Mathematics–Juvenile literature.
Classification: LCC QA40.5 R44 2017 | DDC 510.23–dc23

Published in 2017 by
Gareth Stevens Publishing
111 East 14th Street, Suite 349
New York, NY 10003

Picture credits: 42 U.S. Navy photo by Aviation Warfare Systems Operator 2nd Class William S.
Stevens. All other images from Shutterstock and NASA. 13b InnaFelker; 38 Carine06; 39b Jason
and Bonnie Grower; 41b Maxim Petrichuk; 44 Ververidis Vasilis;45t Darren Brode/Shutterstock.
com

Every effort has been made to trace and contact copyright holders. If there are any inadvertent
omissions we apologise to those concerned, and would be grateful to be notified of any
corrections that should be incorporated in future reprints or editions of this book.

Printed in the United States of America
CPSIA compliance information: Batch CS16GS:
For further information contact Gareth Stevens, New York, New York at 1-800-542-2595.

Contents

MATH IS A LANGUAGE WE ALL UNDERSTAND

Math can help us work out how many days there are until the holidays or how tall we are. But most of all, it helps us make sense of the world. And it's the same language everywhere.

Building blocks of math

People sometimes describe mathematics as a language. It's not really a language that people speak in the street, like English or Japanese, but it does have many things in common with spoken languages. You can think of complicated calculations as books, and simpler ones as words. And the "letters" that lie at the heart of this language are the numbers!

Things that count

Try getting by without using number words to describe things around you. Instead of saying "four trees," you might say "tree tree tree tree." That works pretty well if you're counting small amounts, but it's no good as a way of describing anything larger. Number systems help us solve that problem.

THERE ARE ABOUT 6,500 DIFFERENT LANGUAGES SPOKEN AROUND THE WORLD, BUT NEARLY EVERYONE CAN READ THIS: 0, 1, 2, 3, 4, 5, 6, 7, 8, 9.

Around the world

We can rely on math even when our surroundings are unfamiliar. Imagine visiting a new country—the language may be different, but you will see that the money has its value in numbers as well as words, the prices in stores are a clear amount, and you can recognize your hotel room number. Math will help you get to know your new surroundings.

Did You Know

We know of only one language with no "number words." Its speakers live deep in the Amazon jungle.

Tiny differences

Really big numbers help us work with huge amounts, such as the number of stars in the sky or a computer's memory. But numbers can also shed light on tiny amounts. These might be describing small lengths, like the size of germs. Numbers can also divide time into tiny fragments— which is useful when judging how fast a sprinter has run.

STONE AGE PEOPLE WERE GREAT AT MATH

Counting must have been one of the first skills our ancestors learned. Counting the number of animals in a herd, or the number of moons until the end of the summer, was vital to human survival.

Let's see. If both fish are swimming at 10 feet per second...

The hunt for math

Counting is the foundation of many math skills. If our ancestors could count then they could probably multiply, use fractions, understand geometrical shapes, and make accurate estimates. Getting these things right was hugely important.

The Sumerian people developed the first number symbols around the same time they wrote their first alphabet: about 5,500 years ago.

Seeds of knowledge

As people moved from hunting to farming, they needed more complicated math. They started to work with larger numbers than just "two deer" or "six salmon." Farmers had to decide how much of their crop could be eaten and how much should be saved to plant next year. Bartering developed, which encouraged people to develop a sense of the value of an object.

How many handfuls of seed does it take to plant a field?

Tally ho!

Before most people could read or write, pieces of bone or wood helped them keep a tally, or count, of things. The earliest tally sticks date back more than 30,000 years and have been found in Africa, Europe, and Asia. More recent sticks—from about 1,000 years ago—helped buyers and sellers work out prices. Some people (like prisoners!) still use tally marks to keep track of things.

Ancient times tables

Bamboo strips uncovered in 2014 showed that Chinese people were doing multiplication more than 2,200 years ago. As well as showing how to multiply numbers up to 100, the bamboo had instructions on how to work with fractions. These marks helped villagers to divide portions of grain for use in the winter months.

FRACTIONS CAN BE BEAUTIFUL

Fractions are a simple way of expressing some of the wonders of the world around you. It was something the ancient Egyptians knew well!

> This hat makes me look divine.

Pharaoh fractions

The sculpted head of Nefertiti, royal wife of Egyptian pharaoh Akhenaton, was made more than 3,000 years ago. The ancient Egyptians believed that their rulers would have a godlike beauty. And that beauty could best be represented with **geometry**, the branch of math devoted to shapes and angles. In particular, they tried to produce harmony, a balance between different parts of a design. This comparison can be written as a fraction.

Taking shape

To compare the distance from Nefertiti's nose to chin (call it "a") with the larger distance of chin to hat brim ("b"), you could write "a/b," which is also a fraction. Then to compare "b" with the overall height of the head plus hat ("c"), you'd write "b/c." If you plugged in the real measurements, you'd find that $a/b = b/c$. Awesome!

The Great Sphinx has been showing math in action for 4,500 years.

YOU CAN THINK OF THE LINE BETWEEN THE TOP AND BOTTOM NUMBERS IN A FRACTION AS ANOTHER WAY OF SAYING "DIVIDED BY."

Large-scale design

The Egyptian fascination with fractions, angles, and proportions went far beyond the small-scale design of statues and headdresses. The Egyptians were builders on a huge scale, producing temples, tombs, and monuments to honor their pharaohs and gods. Designs of one construction would often be "echoed" in another nearby, with elements linked with similar angles. The overall effect demonstrated harmony and a mathematical perfection—like that of the heavens.

Egyptian fractions

All Ancient Egyptian fractions were "unitary" and were expressed as one divided by something else. So an Egyptian fraction could be $\frac{1}{2}$, $\frac{1}{3}$, or $\frac{1}{10}$ but not $\frac{2}{5}$ or $\frac{7}{10}$. To add up, you simply combined fractions of different amounts. So to make $\frac{3}{4}$ you could show $\frac{1}{2} + \frac{1}{4}$.

Division made easy

Egyptian fractions might seem clumsy in some ways, but they can be helpful when you try to divide things in real life. Imagine you want to split 7 pizzas between 10 people. Do you divide each pizza into 10 parts and give each person 7 slices? If we look at Egyptian fractions, they show that $\frac{7}{10}$ is the same as $\frac{1}{2} + \frac{1}{5}$. Now we know to cut 5 pizzas in half and to cut the remaining 2 pizzas into five slices each.

9

THE ROMANS USED LETTERS FOR NUMBERS

Did Roman emperors count on their fingers? The Roman numbering system might well have started off like that, with people copying the shapes they saw as they wrote.

Pointing the finger

No matter how complicated numbers can get, we need to be able to represent them clearly. So it's easy to imagine how the Romans would have used something that everyone has: fingers. Just like children counting small numbers on their fingers, the Romans marked "I" (their number "1") down like one finger, "II" like two fingers and "III" like three fingers. Their sign for five— "V"—is the shape a hand makes when you hold up five fingers.

Roman numerals

Lovely letters

The Romans used other letters such as "C" and "M" to represent higher numbers. By combining the letters in different ways they could express almost any number. But using Roman **numerals** meant that adding up was a difficult and time-consuming process. Like many other people, the Romans used the abacus to help them calculate.

No need to write?

Some people have found ways to work out calculations without writing anything down. One of the oldest tools is the abacus. This is a counting frame with rows of beads that slide up and down. The rows represent ones, tens, hundreds, and so on. Expert abacus users can sometimes do calculations faster than a calculator.

Listen to the numbers

Computers might soon make writing numbers down far less important. We can already speak to a computer and let it write, without having to type. A computer can listen to a math problem, solve it, and tell you the answer without you ever having to write down a single number.

ARABIC NUMBERS ARE USED EVERYWHERE

When it comes to doing complicated calculations, Roman numerals are slow and clumsy. Was there a better method?

Making life easier

A numeral is simply a quick way of expressing a number. Today, we use the symbols "0" to "9" to express numbers, and these are called **Arabic numerals**. This system was developed in India, in about AD 500.

Trading up

Traders—people who buy and sell things—need to do complicated calculations quickly. Arabic traders soon saw the advantage of the Indian system. They helped to spread these numerals around the world.

Naming numbers

Numbers don't have to be expressed in numerals. We could use the words "ten thousand two hundred and sixty-seven" but this is time-consuming to write and not easy to work with. When a number is written down in numerals, it can be understood whatever language you speak.

SPEAKERS OF HEBREW AND ARABIC READ LETTERS FROM RIGHT TO LEFT, BUT NUMBERS FROM LEFT TO RIGHT.

Did You Know

In some languages, the words for numbers still refer to fingers and hands.

Counting in the Sotho language is as easy as looking at your hands.

Numerals everywhere

All over the world, people do advanced calculations with Arabic numerals. But when they are speaking, the language they use often has its origin in ancient terms for numbers.

Modern hand-prints

In the Sotho language of southern Africa, the word for "5" is "complete the hand," and "6" is "jump," meaning "jump to the other hand." The Klamath people, Native Americans from the Pacific coast, use similar terms that remind them of pressing their hands on the ground.

SOMETIMES "111" MEANS "7"

Well, it does in the binary system, which uses just two symbols, instead of our normal ten symbols. It's tricky for humans but great for computers.

Marching two by two

We normally use ten symbols (0, 1, 2, 3, 4, 5, 6, 7, 8, 9) to write numbers. When we've used up all of those symbols—say, starting at 0 and going up to 9—we call the next number "10." The "1" goes up with each new set of ten, until it becomes "100." It's called **Base** 10. The binary system uses just two symbols (0, 1) before starting over each time. You end up with numbers with only 0s and 1s in them.

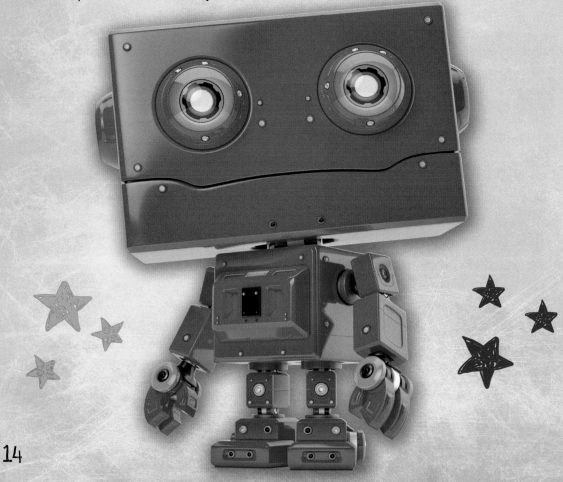

Back to basics

Computers store and send information in tiny bursts of energy. Like a light switch, this energy can be turned on or switched off. That's where the binary system suits computers. Their language is written in a series of 0s and 1s, guiding a computer to turn on or off these signals at super-high speed.

Decimal number	Binary number
1	1
2	10
3	11
4	100
5	101
6	110
7	111
8	1000
9	1001
10	1010

Bits and bytes

A computer "bit" is the smallest unit of data computers use—either a 0 or a 1. Things move up from there. A byte is 8 bits, a kilobyte is 1,000 bytes ... and the numbers keep growing.

THE WORD "BINARY" COMES FROM THE LATIN WORD "BINARIUS," MEANING "TWO TOGETHER."

Bigger and faster

Think about how hard it was to do simple arithmetic when you started school. As you learned more, you found it easier to work quickly, and with bigger numbers. Computers have "grown up" in the same way. The first home computers had memories measured in kilobytes. Now computers have memories of **gigabytes** (each gigabyte is 1,073,741,824 bytes), allowing them to do just about anything you can think of!

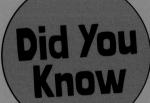
ONE THIRD OF ALL NUMBERS BEGIN WITH "1"

Numbers sometimes behave in strange ways. But there is always a logical explanation for the patterns we see.

Low numbers are winners

If you had time to look at lots of groups of numbers, you would find something very odd. Almost one third of numbers would begin with the digit 1. About another third of numbers would begin with the digits 2 or 3. Only 5% of numbers would begin with the digit 9. This odd fact is known as Benford's Law.

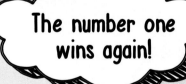

The number one wins again!

Lots of lists

Benford's Law can be found in all sorts of data. It is true when looking at the height of skyscrapers, the length of rivers, electricity bills, addresses, and the population of cities. However, it does not work if the data is limited in some way. Benford's Law would not apply if you looked at the age of children in a class.

The Monty Hall Problem

Monty Hall was the host of the TV game show *Let's Make a Deal*. Mathematicians came up with a puzzle based on the program and called it the Monty Hall Problem. Imagine three doors. Behind two of the doors are goats and behind the other is a car (that's the prize you want to win.) You pick one of the doors. Your host then opens one of the other doors to reveal a goat and then asks you if you want to swap doors. Do you stick with your original choice or do you swap to the other door?

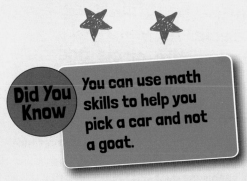

Did You Know

You can use math skills to help you pick a car and not a goat.

The answer is obvious

It seems as though both doors have an equal chance of containing the car. In fact, by swapping to the other door you improve your chances of winning. When you chose your original door you had a ⅓ chance of winning. If you choose to switch doors, you then have a ⅔ chance of winning. This is because the door the host opens is not random; it is <u>never</u> the door the contestant chose and it <u>always</u> contains a goat.

And not just a pie. You can use **pi** to measure the distance around any circle. All you need is two numbers—the width across the circle and the number pi.

A MATHEMATICAL CONSTANT IS ALWAYS THE SAME, BUT IS USED TO HELP MANY DIFFERENT CALCULATIONS.

Constant help

The length around a circle is called its **circumference** and its width is called its **diameter**. More than 3,500 years ago, people in Egypt and China noted that dividing the circumference by the diameter always came up with the same number, just over 3. We now call this special number pi, which is how we spell the Greek letter π. Pi is the most famous example of a constant, or unchanging, number.

Just resting in this circumference...

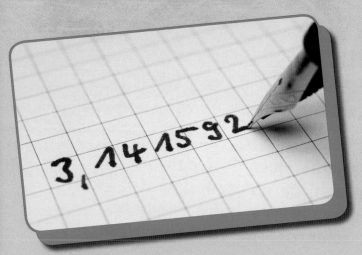

Calculating pi

The best way to find out the value of pi is to take a really accurate measure of a circumference and divide it by the diameter. It would be great if the answer came out as a whole number, or even one where the **decimal places** stop. But it just keeps on going... and going. That puts pi in a special math category—it's known as an **irrational number**. This means that it can't be expressed neatly as a fraction. Some people round pi to the fraction $^{22}/_7$, but that's just an estimate... and starts to go wrong after about the third decimal place.

MATHEMATICIANS CALCULATED PI TO 10 TRILLION DECIMAL PLACES IN 2011.

Out of this world

You can use pi to work out the circumference of a sphere, which is really a circle in three dimensions: length, width, and height. The widest part of a sphere (like the equator running around Earth) is really a circle. That's how scientists can calculate the circumference of distant planets once they've measured how far they are across.

Shaping up

Pi is used to help calculate lots of things beyond just circumferences. For one thing, it can help work out **areas** (the space inside two-dimensional objects like circles) and **volumes** (the space inside three-dimensional objects like spheres). You can use pi to measure any object that has a circular base—even the volume of ice cream that is, or was, in your cone.

19

A STARFISH HAS FIVE LINES OF SYMMETRY

We call something symmetrical if it can be flipped, sliced through, or rotated, and still look the same. Understanding **symmetry** helps engineers with their designs, and some of the best inspiration comes from nature.

Going for a spin

The starfish is an ideal example of rotational symmetry. Imagine finding one on the beach. You could carefully pick it up and move it a one-fifth turn (that's where the rotation is coming in) and put it down again. It would still look the same. And you could do that five times and get the same result. But you'd fail if you tried to do the same thing with an oyster shell or a lobster.

MOST PEOPLE'S FACES ARE NOT QUITE SYMMETRICAL, DESPITE WHAT WE MIGHT THINK.

Natural symmetry

The starfish is an example of symmetry in nature. We come across many other examples of symmetry every day, from the patterns of a cat's coat to our own bodies (both halves would look similar if we were sliced down the middle). Sometimes people "repay this compliment," planting gardens to display perfect symmetry.

Formal gardens owe as much to math as to biology.

Mirror images

Although symmetry can become very complicated and advanced, it's also one of the first math concepts that children understand. The most basic symmetry, called reflective symmetry, is about one line of symmetry. Think of it next time you look in the mirror.

Did You Know

Soccer players calculate the movement of a truncated icosahedron.

Check out my icosahedron kicking skills!

On the ball math

A soccer ball looks like a sphere, but really it is a shape of 32 sides, made up of **pentagons** and **hexagons** which slot together neatly. Imagine a solid shape with 20 triangular faces (this is called an icosahedron). If you cut off (truncate) the 12 corners of the icosahedron you wind up with 12 pentagons and 20 hexagons. In other words, a soccer ball!

The distances between objects in the universe are so big that we call huge numbers "astronomical." But we also have ways of measuring those distances without running out of zeroes.

PROXIMA CENTAURI, THE NEAREST STAR TO OUR SUN, IS 4.24 LIGHT-YEARS AWAY.

Easier units

The best way to "get a handle" on those distances is to use the speed of light, which is 983,571,056 feet per second. Then calculate how far that same light would travel in a year (a **light-year**). You'd need to multiply that big number by 60 (to find a light-minute), then 60 (hour), then 24 (day), and then 365. That means a light-year is 31,039,143,016,731,900 feet, or about 5.88 trillion miles.

Did You Know

The sun is eight light-minutes away from Earth.

Crooked orbits

Most planets have orbits that are ellipses, like slightly flattened circles. Earth's distance from the sun varies from 91.5 million miles to 94.5 million miles each year. Other planets' orbits vary even more.

Vast distances

Earth sits about 93 million miles from the sun. That's a huge number, but that same distance is just a tiny fraction of the distance from the sun to Neptune, the outermost planet in our solar system. And that distance is nothing compared to the distances between stars and galaxies. The zeroes would spill off the page if we kept using miles. So that's why light-years are so handy.

Some telescopes "see" things 100 million light-years away.

The right angle

The night sky is like a semicircle, which can be measured in angles (degrees, minutes, and seconds). Scientists use those angles to calculate distances between Earth and stars. They compare the position of the star at two different times, six months apart. The more distant the star, the less its apparent position will change.

To infinity and beyond?

If the universe has no outer edge, it just goes on and on and on. That boundless idea, or infinity, is also the "destination" of decimals that go on and on, like pi.

NIAGARA FALLS FILLS 7,500 TUBS A SECOND

But only if you could line up all the bathtubs. The official figure for the flow of Niagara Falls is 750,000 gallons per second.

Go with the flow

That's a lot of tubs. Or gallons. Both measurements are useful to scientists. It's important to be able to express the amount using precise terms such as "gallons" but also to find terms that make the amount easier to picture and understand (bathtubs).

Keeping it "real"

Most people wouldn't answer, "Oh, about 5 feet" if someone asked how tall their new refrigerator was. They'd probably say "a bit taller than my dad (or brother)" to give a clearer picture of the height. We like to use familiar images as measurements in conversation, which is why amounts are often compared to football fields, buses, or even Olympic swimming pools.

Heavens above

Measurements that seem too big to understand are sometimes described as being "astronomical"—referring to the vast distances in space. It can be helpful to use models that depict distances and objects on a manageable scale. Some 18th-century models of the solar system were like works of art.

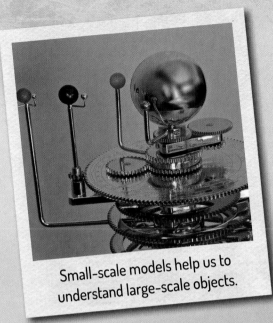

Small-scale models help us to understand large-scale objects.

THE FIRST KNOWN MECHANICAL MODEL OF THE HEAVENS WAS BUILT IN GREECE ABOUT 2,300 YEARS AGO.

I hope no one's going to be taller than 2 inches!

"Scaling up"

Architects also find it easier to work when they have a clear picture of the building they are working on. They do this by creating scale models that are in the same proportion to the finished work. You don't want to build a skyscraper in an office. But a model 2 feet tall would be a useful way of demonstrating its design and features.

A BUTTERFLY'S WINGS CAN CAUSE HURRICANES

Then again, they might not. That uncertainty has led to the rise of a new branch of mathematics. It's known as "chaos theory" because it deals with things that are hard to predict.

UNPREDICTABILITY LIES AT THE HEART OF CHAOS THEORY. THAT'S WHY NO TWO SPORTING MATCHES ARE EXACTLY ALIKE, EVEN IF BOTH TEAMS KEEP THE SAME LINEUPS.

The "Butterfly Effect"

Until the beginning of the 20th century, people believed that all natural actions could be predicted if you had the right information. But a new theory arose, suggesting that even the smallest change in a condition (such as whether or not a butterfly flapped its wings) could lead to huge changes in outcomes (such as whether storms developed on the other side of the world). People described this as the "butterfly effect," using the flapping wings as the example.

Chaos theory helps us predict the "random" behavior of crowds.

Chaos theory

The butterfly effect was just an interesting idea... until the early 1960s. A computer expert with an interest in weather, Edward Lorenz, was setting up programs to predict weather. He noticed that if there was a tiny difference (as little as a millionth decimal place) at the start of a program, the result would change dramatically... maybe even causing "chaos"!

Test the theory

You're probably demonstrating chaos theory today. Would you have chosen that same cereal bowl if your brother had emptied the dishwasher? And would he have emptied the dishwasher if his football game had finished on time? And would the game have ended on time if the referee hadn't been stuck in traffic?

Did You Know Chaos theory is used in medicine.

Medical math

Many things in the human body operate "like clockwork." Even before we are born, our hearts beat in a predictable rhythm. But sometimes a baby's heartbeat becomes irregular, and it's hard to know why. Doctors are now using chaos theory to work backward, and to find a reason for the abnormal heartbeat without operating. After all, chaos theory tells us that events are not unpredictable if we have enough data.

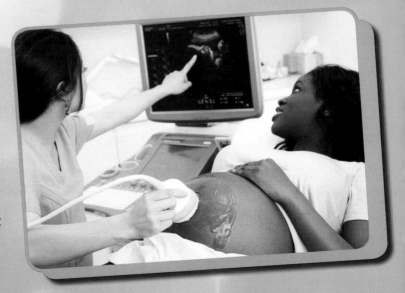

SOME SEEDS GROW IN A MATH PATTERN

Sunflowers might seem to have a crowded collection of seeds, but they grow in an important mathematical arrangement. And those same patterns appear in many other plants—and animals.

Natural sequence

The **Fibonacci sequence** is what you get if you start out 0, 1, and then add the last two numbers to get the next one: 1, 2, 3, 5, 8, 13, and so on. Mathematicians have divided the numbers in the sequence by the previous one. After the first three pairs (which divide neatly), you wind up with numbers that get pretty close to 1.618—but not quite exactly. That "golden ratio," like pi, can't be reduced to a neat fraction.

Do I detect a pattern?

A sunflower needs to cluster as many seeds as possible into its blossom. It needs to "place one, then turn" before placing the next. If its fraction of a turn is exact—like ¼ for example—the seeds would be arranged in straight lines outward. "Turning" 1.618 times crams the most seeds into that small area.

Getting the most

The sunflower packs in seeds to get the most in a small area. Other plants have Fibonacci patterns in their leaf arrangements. And the number of branches (or roots going down) that develop on a tree follow a sequence of 1, 2, 3, 5, 8, 13... as the best way to capture light.

Animal designs

Shellfish and snails have hard outer shells that spiral outward from a central point. Imagine a rectangle with the longer side 1.618 times longer than the shorter side. And then drawing another rectangle so that the first "longer side" becomes the shorter side. And again, and again. Curving out from corner to corner would produce the exact same spiral.

PRIME NUMBERS HELP ANIMALS TO SURVIVE

Prime numbers can only be divided by themselves, or one. And mathematicians aren't the only ones interested in them. Insects have entire life cycles based on prime numbers.

WHEN PERIODIC CICADAS HATCH, THEY REALLY ARRIVE IN NUMBERS—SOMETIMES 3.5 MILLION IN EVERY 2.5 ACRES (1 HA) OF LAND.

Prime-time arrivals

All insects hatch into a larva before emerging as adults—and usually the insects become adults at the same time every year. But periodical cicadas of eastern North America have a much longer gap between each new wave. These locust-like insects emerge either every 13 or 17 years. It's those "periods" of 13 or 17 years that give the insects their name. And it's not a coincidence that 13 and 17 are both prime numbers!

Boom and bust

Having a prime-number gap between appearances gives the cicada a real advantage. And it is all down to the population cycle of its predators. Most animals have years when their population is larger and years when it is smaller. It depends on the amount of food available and how many predators are around.

Cicada with 12-year life cycle

predator with 2-year life cycle: overlap in years 12, 24, 36, 48, and 60	predator with 3-year life cycle: overlap in years 12, 24, 36, 48, and 60

Cicada with 13-year life cycle

predator with 2-year life cycle: overlap in years 26 and 52	predator with 3-year life cycle: overlap in year 39

Avoiding the enemy

Cicadas want to avoid emerging during years when there are many predators. A prime number life cycle is the best way of doing that. It gives the cicada the best chance of emerging in a year when its predators' populations are low. Just look at how often a cicada with a 12-year life cycle coincides with its predators compared to a 13-year cicada. You won't be surprised to hear that there are no 12-year cicadas!

Did You Know The fiddler crab's claw gets stronger every 29.5 days.

Lunar cycles

Male fiddler crabs try to attract mates with their strong snapping claw. But females only want to mate at the full moon or the new moon. This ensures their babies emerge at high tides, when the strong ocean currents will sweep them far away and give them the best chance of survival. So the male crabs put on their best displays once a month. Snap! Snap!

THERMOMETERS USE DIFFERENT ZEROES

If your thermometer reads "zero" then you know it's cold. But that "zero" might be describing a much colder temperature if your thermometer is from another country... or a science lab.

Measuring the world

The **Fahrenheit** temperature scale, used in the United States, sets its zero 32 degrees colder than the freezing point of water. Most other parts of the world measure heat and cold in **Celsius**, where water freezes at zero degrees and boils at 100 degrees. So a temperature of zero is much colder in New York than in London.

A BANANA EXPOSED TO ABSOLUTE ZERO FREEZES HARD ENOUGH TO BE USED AS A HAMMER.

Down to absolute zero

Using water as the starting point (zero) of a temperature makes sense. Most people have seen water freeze and boil. But many scientists use yet another scale, the **Kelvin** scale. The gaps between degrees are the same as in Celsius, but the scale starts at absolute zero and goes up from there. Absolute zero is the temperature where all motion stops, even in the smallest atoms.

Getting negative

The real world is the best way to learn about some difficult math ideas. Some people have a hard time understanding negative numbers, which begin at zero and go "the wrong way." But a temperature of "six below zero" is just another way of saying "negative six."

You don't need to be a math wiz to feel wind chill.

Did You Know

Adding in wind chill explains why you feel colder than the thermometer suggests.

Wind chill

A thermometer accurately measures the temperature of the air, but we also lose heat when it's windy. Scientists have found a method, called wind chill, to describe how cold we feel in certain weather. They combine wind speed with temperature to calculate wind chill. A very windy 25-degree day could have a wind chill of -5 degrees and feel colder than a 20-degree day with no wind.

Imagine a visitor to the US has one cent, and finds a way to double the money she has every day. At first the amounts are small, but watch what happens when numbers meet the "power of powers."

Powering ahead

The increase is based on the power of 2. By the second day, the single cent has become two, or "2 to the power of 1" (2 multiplied by itself once). By the 31st day, it has reached "2 to the power of 30": 1,073,741,824 cents, or $10,737,418.24. This rapid increase is an example of **exponential growth**: You multiply a number by something to get the next one.

EXPONENTIAL GROWTH IS MUCH MORE RAPID THAN LINEAR GROWTH, WHERE THE SAME AMOUNT IS ADDED EACH TIME.

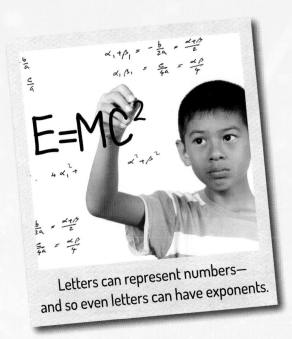

Letters can represent numbers— and so even letters can have exponents.

Writing shortcut

A small number above and to the right of another number is called an **exponent**. It tells us the number of times the lower number is multiplied by itself (or "raised to that power"). So 8^4 is a quick way of writing 8x8x8x8, or "8 raised to the power of four."

RAISING TO THE POWER OF TWO IS ALSO CALLED "SQUARING"; "CUBING" DESCRIBES RAISING TO THE POWER OF THREE.

It's a good thing!

Exponential growth can be helpful. Banks pay savers interest on their money each year. It's a percentage of the savings, including the interest that's already been added. That's called compound interest.

Did You Know

An Australian farmer imported 24 English rabbits in 1859. Within six years, the rabbit population had multiplied to 22 million.

It's a bad thing!

Exponential growth can also multiply problems. Australia had no native rabbits until people brought them in. The rabbit population grew exponentially. Within a few years, rabbits were out of control and damaging farms across the country.

35

TWO PEOPLE IN A CLASS SHARE A BIRTHDAY

There's really a "probably" in there: two people probably share a birthday. Math tells us that in any room of 23 people, it's more likely than not that two people were born on the same day.

Number crunching

"More likely than not" means that there's a better than 50 percent chance that two people will share a birthday. In fact, it's a 50.05 percent chance, but it takes a lot of detailed calculation to reach that answer. The hard part is knowing where to start. Remember: It's not just you finding a match from 22 other people, it's everyone. That means that there are 253 pairs that might give a match.

AN OCTOPUS KNOWN AS PAUL CORRECTLY PREDICTED THE OUTCOME OF GERMANY'S SIX WORLD CUP SOCCER MATCHES IN 2010... COMPLETELY BY CHANCE!

Important guidance

Many examples of **probability**, like the shared birthdays, seem hard to believe. But this branch of math isn't just looking at things that are likely to happen. It calculates what could happen. That ability to calculate possibilities is very important. It helps us build up stocks of medicine, keep machinery safe and work out how much money to set aside for all sorts of emergencies.

Family predictions

Some of the most familiar examples of probability are all around you. Genetics, the study of what parents pass on to their children, uses probability to make some general predictions. What is the chance you will have a left-handed child? Genetics tell us it's one in 10 if both parents are right-handed, about three in 10 if both parents are left-handed.

Left-handed? What are the chances of that?

Did You Know

You can win at rock-paper-scissors without being a mind reader.

Playground probability

People can combine the math skills of probability with psychology (the study of how people behave) to make some surprising predictions. Even familiar games of "chance" (luck) can be studied to gain an advantage. For example, a winner of rock-paper-scissors tends to use the same choice for the next turn, while the loser moves to the next choice.

YOU CAN WIN AND LOSE IN TENNIS

The scoring in tennis can lead to some odd results. And it's not just sports and games that seem to break the rules of mathematics... or common sense.

Settling scores

It's simple to work out the winner in most sports. The player or team that scores the most points wins, whether they're playing football, basketball, or baseball. But a tennis match is broken down into sets and games... and then points. Both players try to win each point, but those points don't count directly toward overall victory. So, in a match scored 1-6, 7-5, 7-5, the winner would have won one fewer game than the loser (15 compared to 16).

THE LONGEST TENNIS MATCH EVER TOOK MORE THAN 11 HOURS. JOHN ISNER DEFEATED NICOLAS MAHUT 6-4, 3-6, 6-7, 7-6, 70-68.

Quick calculations

Sports and games often call for math skills. Bridge and poker players keep track of which cards have been played to work out what remains. They then use probability to guess what is likely to happen next.

A bridge player calculates the best way to score points.

THE FEWEST NUMBER OF DARTS THAT CAN BE THROWN TO WIN A GAME IS NINE. YOU NEED TO HIT TRIPLE 20 SIX TIMES, THEN TRIPLE 17, TRIPLE 18, AND DOUBLE 18.

Bull's-eye

Darts players need to be good at subtraction as well as accurate throwing. The dartboard is divided into numbered sections, and if you hit a number it is taken off your score. You are aiming to get from 501 points to zero. You need to subtract quickly to work out your new score, and decide which number is best to aim at.

Majority rules?

Many countries decide their government by counting the votes separately in different areas. The political party with the most of these smaller victories wins overall. But it might have won by just a handful of votes in each of its "victories," and had hardly any votes in the others. Some United States presidents, including President George W. Bush, have been elected with fewer votes than their opponents.

SHARKS CAN SMELL ONE IN A MILLION

A shark's sense of smell is so acute that it can detect one part blood within a million parts of water. That leads to a **ratio** of 1:1,000,000.

Scary numbers

A ratio is a way of comparing two numbers of a similar kind. This ratio 1:1,000,000 is comparing two liquids—blood and seawater. The most "mathematical" way to express a ratio is with numerals (such as 1:1,000,000 for blood and seawater). But sometimes it's easier for people to understand—or get scared by—ratios if we express them differently. One million gallons of water is quite hard to picture, but you could express the ratio using something familiar, such as "sharks can detect half a gallon of blood in an Olympic-sized swimming pool."

RATIOS CAN BE REDUCED, JUST LIKE FRACTIONS. A RATIO OF 12:48 IS THE SAME AS 6:24, 3:12, 2:8 OR 1:4.

All in the mix

We come across ratios all the time, even if we don't recognize them. At the supermarket we compare the price per pound of products to decide on the best deal. At school we might tally up the number of left- and right-handed students. If, for example, there are three left-handers and 27 right-handers, then the ratio is 3:27.

Fair rate of pay

Ratios also play a part in the ways that people are rewarded for their work. People are often paid a certain amount per hour or week. These ratios are called hourly or weekly rates. And companies usually provide holidays, often considered as a number of days per year—the more days the better!

Did You Know

A cyclist must pick the right ratio to go uphill.

What goes up....

Bicycle gears operate as ratios. If you're climbing a hill, you use a small gear (with fewer teeth) by the pedals and a big gear (with lots of teeth) at the back. The number of teeth might have a ratio of 11:44. It's pretty easy to push the bike a quarter of a rear-wheel rotation, which is how far one pedal-gear rotation pushes the rear gear. But it doesn't get you as far as the (more tiring) 22:44 combination.

Did You Know

TWO HUNDRED TONS OF METAL CAN FLOAT

A huge ship made of steel and weighing more than 200,000 tons can float as easily as a cork. But a steel spoon will sink. Where does math come into it?

Floating ratios

Ratios—that's where. Things float when they are less dense than the fluid surrounding them. And **density** is all about a specific ratio: **mass** to volume (or the weight of an object compared to the space it fills). The volume of the ship includes its spaces, which weigh very little. And that lowers its density. The spoon has a small mass, but a tiny volume.

THE "SEAWISE GIANT," THE LARGEST SHIP EVER BUILT, WEIGHED 724,239 TONS.

Over the edge?

Buoyancy, the force that keeps things floating, depends on how much water an object displaces, or pushes away. You can see that displacement when you get in the bath and the water rises... and sometimes spills out. The buoyancy force equals the weight of the water that's been displaced.

Vela

SIRIUS STAR

Up and down

If a supertanker can float because the ratio of its mass and volume works, then what about a submarine? Again, it's about ratios, but ones that can be adjusted. A sub that's climbing or on the surface has tubes filled with air. If it needs to dive, the crew pumps water into those tubes, increasing the mass in the ratio.

I'll just lean against this chair...

Other ratios

Ratios are often the best way to prepare a government's "report card." Citizens expect their governments to raise some ratios, such as "teachers:pupils in schools" or "doctors:1,000 people in a country." Other ratios, such as "crimes:10,000 people," should be reduced if a government wants to remain in power.

Did You Know Gravity is a weak force, even on Earth. We can overcome it just by standing up!

May the force be with you

All objects create **gravity**, but the amount depends on the mass of the object. Most objects create only a very tiny amount of gravity, but the mass of Earth is huge and we can certainly feel the gravity created by our planet! The moon has one sixth of Earth's mass. That means the ratio of its gravity compared to Earth's is 1:6. Seen another way, it tells us that moving objects can go six times further on the moon than on Earth before gravity pulls them down.

EVEN EXPERTS EXPECT ERRORS

Predictions based on math are bound to be true, right? Well, not always. Mathematicians are aware that in the real world, all data has built-in mistakes.

Margin of error

The best way to predict an election winner would be to ask every voter beforehand. That's impossible, so you choose a sample—a smaller group that matches the overall population. Math experts then work out two things: first, which party is likely to win the election and second, the "margin of error." This calculates how representative the sample is, and so how likely it is that the sample group can predict the result.

The bigger the better

To be representative, a sample group must match the general population. Statisticians must work out how to ensure a "match." They try to ensure their sample is representative in terms of age, sex, location, education, and wealth. Usually, the larger the sample the more representative it is.

Market research

Sample groups are also used by companies to plan new products and advertisements. This is called market research. However, sometimes market research gets things very wrong. The Ford Motor Company introduced a new model, the Edsel, in 1958. It had tested people's likes and dislikes in a car to come up with the design. But the car proved unpopular and production stopped two years later.

COMPANIES SOMETIMES LOSE MILLIONS BY MISCALCULATING PUBLIC OPINION.

The same statistics can be presented in different ways.

Did You Know

Statistics can use numbers to trick people.

Tricked by numbers?

Statistics can be misleading. It's usually not the numbers that are false. Instead it's the way in which they're presented. This could be something like not starting a graph at zero to make differences look bigger, or it could be the wording. A "100 percent increase in injuries in one year" might simply mean that one person (out of 12,000) was injured one year and two people were injured the next.

45

Glossary

Arabic numerals The number symbols 0, 1, 2, 3, etc., that we use today.

area The space inside 2-dimensional objects.

base The numbers that are used in a counting system. For example, base 10 uses numbers 0 to 9, base 2 (the binary system) uses only two numbers, 0 and 1.

bit In computers, the smallest unit of data (either 0 or 1), A byte is 8 bits.

Celsius A temperature scale that uses the freezing point of water as 0 degrees, and the boiling point as 100 degrees.

chaos theory The branch of mathematics that deals with complex systems that are sensitive to tiny changes.

circumference The distance around the edge of a circle.

decimal place In the decimal system, the position of a number in relation to the decimal point which determines its value.

density The weight of an object compared to the amount of space it fills.

diameter The distance of a straight line from side to side passing through the center of a circle.

exponent A number that says how many times to use that number in a multiplication. It is written as a small number to the right and above the base number.

exponential growth Growth of a system in proportion to its size—so the bigger the number the bigger the growth.

Fahrenheit A temperature scale that uses a zero that is 32 degrees colder than the freezing point of water.

Fibonacci sequence The number sequence 0, 1, 1, 2, 3, 5, 8, etc., in which each number is the sum of the previous two numbers.

geometry The branch of math that deals with points, lines, shapes, and angles.

gigabyte A unit of data used by computers, equivalent to 1,073,741,824 bytes.

gravity The force that attracts bodies toward the center of Earth.

hexagon A six-sided shape.

irrational number A number that can't be expressed neatly as a fraction.

Kelvin A temperature scale that starts at absolute zero—the temperature at which all motion stops.

light-year The distance that light travels in a year.

mass A measure of how much matter there is in an object.

numeral A symbol that stands for a number.

pentagon A five-sided shape.

pi The number reached by dividing the circumference of a circle by its diameter (approximately 3.14). It is a constant, or unchanging, number.

prime number A number that can only be divided by itself, or one.

probability The branch of mathematics that studies how likely something is to happen.

ratio A way of comparing two numbers of a similar kind.

statistics The branch of mathematics that deals with collecting, organizing, and presenting numbers.

symmetry Describes a shape that stays the same whether you flip, slide, or turn it.

volume The space inside 3-dimensional objects.

Further Information: Websites

http://www.learner.org/interactives/dailymath/
This website demonstrates how math plays a huge part in our everyday lives, from cooking to playing games.

http://www.mathgametime.com/
This fun website features math-related games to reinforce a variety of math skills.

http://www.math.com/
This valuable website covers a variety of math subjects for a range of grade levels.

http://figurethis.nctm.org/index.html
This NCTM website features real-world math challenges to inspire learning.

http://www.coolmath.com/
This website offers cool activities, games, and animated demonstrations for a dynamic learning experience.

Publisher's note to educators and parents: Our editors have carefully reviewed these websites to ensure that they are suitable for students. Many websites change frequently, however, and we cannot guarantee that a site's future contents will continue to meet our high standards of quality and educational value. Be advised that students should be closely supervised whenever they access the Internet.

Further Information: Books

Clemens, Meg, Glenn Clemens, and Sean Clemens. *The Everything Kids' Math Puzzles Book*. Avon, MA: Adams Media, 2003.

DK Children. *Amazing Visual Math*. New York, NY: DK Children, 2014.

Goldsmith, Mike. *How to Be a Math Genius*. New York, NY: DK Children, 2012.

Lee, Martin, and Marcia Miller. *40 Fabulous Math Mysteries Kids Can't Resist*. Jefferson City, MO: Scholastic, Inc., 2001.

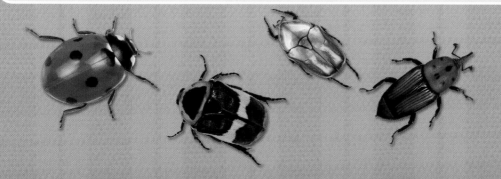

Index